Rubber Band
MANIA

Crafts, Activities, Facts, and Fun!

by Amanda Formaro

studio fun BOOKS

White Plains, New York • Montréal, Quebec • Bath, United Kingdom

Rubber Band Mania

Art Director: Karen Viola
Designer: Stephanie Weinberger
Editor: Elizabeth Bennett

Published by Studio Fun International, Inc.
44 South Broadway, White Plains, NY 10601 U.S.A. and
Studio Fun International Limited,
The Ice House, 124-126 Walcot Street, Bath UK BA1 5BG
All rights reserved.
Studio Fun Books is a trademark of Studio Fun International, Inc.,
a division of The Reader's Digest Association, Inc.
Printed in China.
Conforms to ASTM F963 and EN 71
10 9 8 7 6 5 4 3 2 1
HH2/03/14

Photo images by Amanda Formaro with the exception of the following:

Cover: ©NY-P/Shutterstock.com (ball), ©Pavel L Photo and Video/Shutterstock.com (boy); Page 4 (hand with chopsticks): ©Andrei Shumskiy/Shutterstock.com;
Page 7: ©Denys Prykhodov/Shutterstock.com; Page 8: ©Apples Eyes Studio/Shutterstock.com; Page 12: ©vetkit/Shutterstock.com; Page 13:
©STILLFX/Shutterstock.com, ©Zerbor/Shutterstock.com; Page 23: ©Tracy Whiteside/Shutterstock.com; Page 24: ©Africa Studio/Shutterstock.com;
Page 28: ©Elnur/Shutterstock.com, ©John Abbate/Shutterstock.com; Page 31: ©Andrey_Kuzmin/Shutterstock.com, ©Taigi/Shutterstock.com; Page 32:
©Andrei Shumskiy/Shutterstock.com; Page 33: ©jason cox/Shutterstock.com, ©NY-P/Shutterstock.com, ©Pavel L Photo and Video/Shutterstock.com,
©photovs/Shuttertock; Page 35: ©Denys Prykhodov/Shutterstock.com, ©Elnur/Shutterstock.com; Page 40: ©Dan kosmayer/Shutterstock.com;
Page 41: ©DenisNata/Shutterstock.com; ©Dan kosmayer/Shutterstock.com; Page 42: ©STILLFX/Shutterstock.com; Page 48: ©leedsn/Shutterstock.com;
Page 49: ©Givaga/Shutterstock.com; Page 51: ©Robynrg/Shutterstock.com; Page 55: ©RAYphotographer/Shutterstock (middle/left), ©Polryaz/Shutterstock
(bottom left), ©Monkey Business Images/Shutterstock.com (bottom right); Page 56: ©Volodymyr Krasyuk/Shutterstock.com;
Page 63: ©Maks Narodenko/Shutterstock.com; Page 67: ©Tracy Whiteside/Shutterstock.com; Page 68: ©sue yassin/Shutterstock.com,
©ppart/Shutterstock.com; Page 72: ©mervas/Shutterstock.com

Page backgrounds and graphics: ©donatas1205, ©J.D.S, ©Ingka D. Jiw, ©pun photo, ©Radiocat, ©Roman Samokhin, ©secondcorner, ©Roman Sigaev,
©Nuttapong Wongcheronkit/Shutterstock.com

Library of Congress Data has been applied for.

Contents

Oh the simple rubber band. Open your mom's junk drawer, or the top drawer of your desk, and you are likely to find a bunch of these stretchy bands. Perhaps you have wondered what rubber bands are good for besides keeping a newspaper rolled up. Or perhaps you have joined the craze and have been making bracelets out of tiny bands for months. Well, either way, this book is for you!

We'll show you amazing ways to make all kinds of bracelets, belts, and more with (and without) a loom. You will learn how to use a rubber band to propel a car across the floor, sail a paper airplane with amazing speed, and shoot a marshmallow into the air. We will show you how to create all kinds of awesome projects and crafts with just a handful of rubber bands and some simple supplies. Filled with awesome facts and fun tips, the ideas in this book will guarantee that you never look at a rubber band the same way again.

Ready to **stretch** your imagination? Well, let's get started!

No skills? No sweat! Look for this symbol for our simplest crafts.

Crafting Rock Star? Look for this symbol for our harder crafts.

5

Chain Bracelets

Making a bunch of colorful bracelets is a snap with this simple method!

What You Need:

✓ A bag of tiny bands in a variety of colors

✓ One plastic c-clip (sometimes they come with the bands, or you can buy them separately at a craft store)

1 Pick out the two colors you want to use. For this example we are using blue and red.

2 Lay a red band on top of a blue band.

3 Loop them through each other and pull tight.

4 Take a red band, fold it in half and slide it through the blue band.

5 Take a blue band, fold it in half and slide it through both loops of the new red band.

6 Repeat steps 4 and 5 until your bracelet is the right length.

7 Slide the c-clip into both loops of your last band. Then slide it into the other end (the first red band).

8 That's it! You've made a bracelet without a loom! Try it with lots of different patterns and color combinations.

IT'S A SNAP

The next time you have a party, or a bunch of friends over, put big fat rubber bands around the drinks that you are serving. Then offer your friends a marker to label their glass. No more mix-ups!

snap FACT!

You may call it a rubber band, but did you know that there are lots of other names for these stretchy bands of rubber? Here are just a few!

✓ elastic band   ✓ lackey band

✓ loop band   ✓ jimmy

✓ gum band   ✓ binder

Finger Loom Bracelet

No loom? No problem! Rubber band bracelets made on a loom are quite the craze these days. But did you know you could easily make colorful rubber band bracelets with just your fingers? Here's how.

What You Need:

✓ A bag of tiny bands in a variety of colors

✓ One plastic c-clip (sometimes they come with the bands, or you can buy them separately at a craft store)

1 Hold your pointer finger and middle finger straight up touching each other. This is your finger loom!

2 Place one end of a rubber band over one finger, twist the rubber band once and place the other end over the second finger, creating a figure eight. You will only make a figure eight this one time.

3 Place a second rubber band over both fingers, keeping it positioned above the figure-eight band.

4 Place a third rubber band over both fingers, keeping it positioned above the second rubber band.

5 Grasp the bottom rubber band from your pointing finger and pull it straight out to the side.

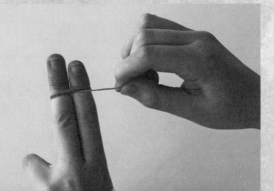

6 Keeping your fingers together, pull that rubber band straight up and over your pointing finger and drop it down between both fingers.

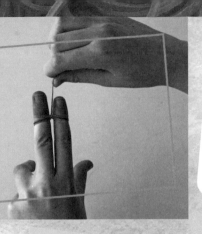

7 Now grasp the bottom rubber band from your middle finger and pull it straight out to the side.

8 Keeping your fingers together, lift it straight up and over your middle finger and drop it in between your two fingers.

10 Repeat steps 5–9 until your bracelet has reached the desired length.

9 Place a new rubber band over both fingers so that it is positioned at the top.

11 Take a c-clip and hook it over the rubber bands that remain on your pointing finger.

12 Hook the other side of the c-clip over the rubber bands that remain on your middle finger.

EXTRA TWIST! The key to a nice tight bracelet is keeping your fingers together as you add bands.

13 Now that your fingers are free, grasp the end of the bracelet without the c-clip. Locate the loose end (the very first rubber band you used) and slip it into the c-clip, closing your bracelet.

14 Make as many bracelets as you want using different colors and patterns!

Fishtail Bracelet Using a FORK

What You Need:
- ✓ Plastic fork
- ✓ Rubber bands (40–60 depending on length)
- ✓ C-clip

You just learned how to make a fishtail bracelet using your fingers, but did you know you can do the same thing with a plastic fork? Now we are going to show you how to use a fork instead of your fingers to do the weaving.

1 Carefully break off the center two tines of your plastic fork.

2 Loop the first rubber band onto the two tines in a figure eight pattern.

3 Loop another rubber band above the figure-eight band.

4 Loop a third rubber band above those other two bands.

5 Grab the right side of the bottom rubber band and stretch it out to the right. Lift it up and over the top of the right tine of the fork and drop it so that it rests on the center of the top band. Repeat on the left side.

6 Place another rubber band on top above the other bands.

7 Repeat steps 5 and 6 until you reach the desired length.

8 Attach a c-clip to the end of the bracelet that is not attached to the fork.

9 Repeat step 5 two more times so that you only have one band remaining on the fork tines.

10 Move one side of the band over to the other side. Both ends of that rubber band should now be on the one tine.

11 Insert your finger through that remaining rubber band so that both ends are on your finger and remove it from the fork tine.

12 Stretch the band and attach the c-clip from the other end of the bracelet.

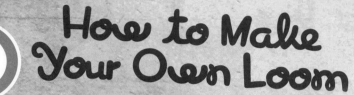

How to Make Your Own Loom

While it's great fun (and easy!) to make rubber band bracelets without using a loom, some designs are more complicated and require one. You don't have to run out to the store, however. Here's how to make one at home!

What You Need:

✓ Corkboard (you can use an old bulletin board if you want!)

✓ 39 pushpins

✓ Ruler

1 Insert a straight row of 13 pushpins into corkboard, spacing them one inch apart. If you want, you can use a ruler to mark the line and the spots for the pins.

2 Make another row of 13 pushpins 1½ inches away from the first row. You should now have two parallel rows of 13 pins.

3 Now you are going to make the center row. It will not line up exactly with the left and right rows. It will have the same number of pins (13) but needs to be offset. So start this row ½ inch before the other two rows. Then space the rest of the pins one inch apart.

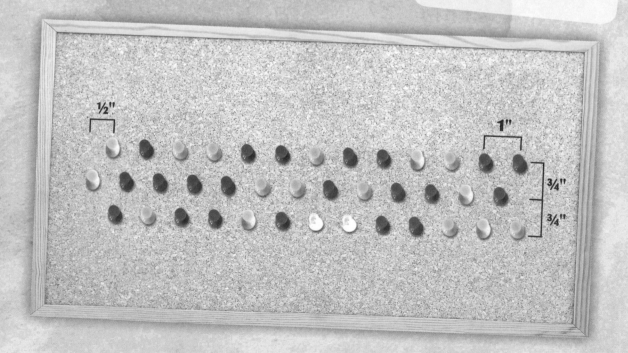

½"   1"   ¾"   ¾"

LOOM BASICS

A few basic terms and tips to help you use a loom like a pro!

PLACEMENT OF LOOM: There should be an arrow on your loom. When starting a bracelet design, that arrow should be pointed away from you. When hooking the design, the loom will be turned around with the arrow pointed toward you. If your loom doesn't have an arrow, start with the pointed end of the loom facing toward you.

USING A CROCHET HOOK: With the hook facing away from you, keep it straight up and down to insert between the peg and band. Tip slightly back toward you to hook bands and lift them off the peg.

C-CLIP: A small c-shaped piece of plastic for connecting the two ends of your bracelet. Sometimes it may be shaped like an S. These hooks usually come with the little bands you buy to use with looms.

DB: When you see this abbreviation, it means doubled bands. You will use two rubber bands together.

PEGS/PINS: The raised round pieces of your loom that you place rubber bands on.

CAP BAND: A band that will be placed around a peg, then twisted to double it, and wrapped around the peg a second time.

TRIPLE CAP BAND: A band that will be wrapped around a peg three times.

BRACE BAND: A triangular shape made by stretching the band from a top peg down to two lower pegs.

HOOK: Using a crochet hook to pull bands from one peg and move them to another peg.

LOOP: Placing a band on one peg and stretching the other end of the band to another peg.

EXTRA TWIST!

The pushpin and corkboard loom is a simple way to make your own loom, but you may find that some of the more difficult designs are harder to make. Your pushpins may pull out with the pressure from the bands. If you want to make a stronger loom, you can use a piece of wood and nails (the kind of nails that have heads). Have an adult help you hammer the nails into the wood using the same pattern of rows we show in the photo on page 12.

13

What You Need:

✓ Homemade loom

✓ Crochet hook

✓ 25 rubber bands

✓ C-clip

Single Chain Bracelet

If you've never made a bracelet on a loom before, this is the design for you. It's the easiest one to make, and once you've mastered it you'll be ready to move onto more detailed designs!

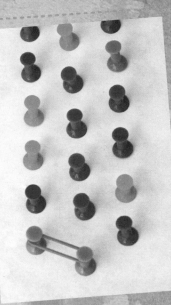

1 Place your homemade loom in front of you.

2 Place a rubber band on the bottom center pin and stretch it up to the bottom left pin.

3 Place a second rubber band onto the bottom left pin and stretch it up to the right, to the second center pin.

4 Repeat steps 2 and 3, creating a zig-zag pattern up the loom until you get to the top.

5 Turn the loom around so the bottom is now at the top.

6 Use your crochet hook to grab the bottom rubber band on the second pin from underneath the rubber band on the first pin.

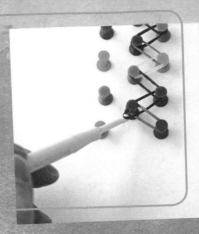

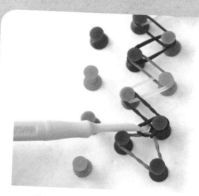

7 Pull the band up and loop it over the next pin up in the zig-zag pattern.

8 Insert your crochet hook through the loops you just created on that last pin, and grab the rubber band below it. Loop it up and over the next pin in the zig-zag pattern.

9 Repeat step 8 until you have reached the end of the bands.

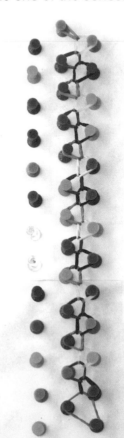

10 Stretch out the last band on the loom and attach a c-clip.

11 Carefully remove the bracelet from the loom and attach the c-clip to the other end of the bracelet.

Fishtail Bracelet

Now that you have your homemade loom, you'll want to make more pretty bracelets! One of the most popular designs, and easiest to make, is the fishtail. This super-simple design will have you cranking out jewelry in no time.

What You Need:

✓ C-clip
✓ Rubber bands (50–60 depending on length)
✓ Homemade loom
✓ Crochet hook

1 Turn your loom sideways and choose two pegs to use that are side by side.

2 Place one end of a rubber band over one peg, twist the rubber band once and place the other end over the second peg, creating a figure eight. You will only make a figure eight this one time.

3 Place a second rubber band over both pegs, keeping it positioned above the figure-eight band.

4 Place a third rubber band over both pegs, keeping it positioned above the second rubber band.

16

5 Using your crochet hook, grab the bottom rubber band from the left peg and pull it straight out to the side. Pull that rubber band straight up and over the left peg and drop it down between the two pegs, resting on the top band.

6 Now grasp the bottom rubber band from the right peg and pull it straight out to the side. Lift it straight up and over the peg and drop it in between the two pegs, resting on the top band.

7 Place a new rubber band over both pegs so that it is positioned at the top.

8 Repeat steps 5–7 until your bracelet has reached the desired length.

9 Take a c-clip and hook it onto the first rubber band loop on the hanging end of your bracelet.

10 Repeat step 5 so that only one rubber band remains on the pegs.

11 Hook the c-clip from the end of the bracelet to the remaining loops on the pegs, closing your bracelet.

snap FACT!

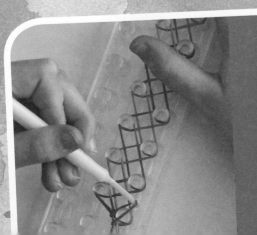

The official Rainbow Loom® was invented in 2010 by a dad named Cheong Choon Ng for his teenage daughters. He noticed that they were making bracelets on their fingers and thought a loom would help. His first loom was made with pushpins and a wooden slab (a lot like our homemade loom!). His loom was so successful that he started a company and the craze took off!

Beaded Fishtail Bracelet

This fun design is one of our favorites! Take the ever popular fishtail and weave in a few beads for a special look. Make it personalized with alphabet beads, too! (We are making this one with green and pink rubber bands, but you can substitute any colors you choose.)

What You Need:

✓ 1 c-clip
✓ 8 pony beads
✓ 14 green rubber bands
✓ 27 pink rubber bands
✓ Homemade loom or store-bought loom*
✓ Crochet hook

*Homemade looms are great for simple bracelets, but you may want to use a store-bought loom for more elaborate patterns.

1 Thread a pink rubber band through the hole of one of the pony beads. Repeat for all remaining beads. Set aside.

2 With your loom turned sideways, choose two pegs (side by side) to use for this bracelet. Loop one end of a green rubber band over one peg, twist it once to create a figure eight pattern, and loop the other end over the second peg. This will be the only rubber band that you twist into a figure eight. Push the figure eight down toward the bottom of the pegs.

3 Add two more green rubber bands onto the pegs above the figure eight.

4 Using your crochet hook from the outside of the left peg, grab the bottom band, bring it up and out over the peg and release it into the center of the top bands. Repeat this step for the right side as well.

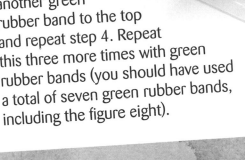

5 Add another green rubber band to the top and repeat step 4. Repeat this three more times with green rubber bands (you should have used a total of seven green rubber bands, including the figure eight).

6 Next add three pink rubber bands using the same process.

7 Now it's time to add a beaded band. Loop both ends of a beaded band over the pegs the same way you did in step 2 and then follow step 4.

9 Repeat steps 7 and 8 seven more times to use all the beads.

8 Add two more pink bands without beads.

10 Continue the fishtail weaving process with the remaining seven green rubber bands.

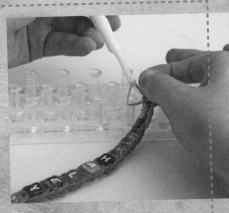

11 After adding the final green rubber band, pull the bottom bands up and over the pegs so that there is only one band remaining on each peg.

12 Carefully grab those two bands with your crochet hook and connect them to the c-clip. Connect the c-clip to the other end of the bracelet to connect it together.

EXTRA TWIST! This beaded bracelet can also be made using the finger loom method (page 8) or the fork loom method (page 10).

SPIRAL BRACELET

Once you've mastered the single chain bracelet and the fishtail pattern, you'll want to give this pretty spiral design a try. It's an easy bracelet to make but you may want to practice the single chain first to get the hang of a store-bought loom.

What You Need:

✓ 16 turquoise rubber bands
✓ 16 pink rubber bands
✓ Loom
✓ Crochet hook

(We have made ours with turquoise and pink rubber bands, but you can substitute any colors you like!)

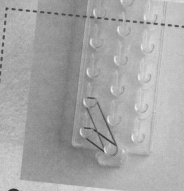

1 Place your loom on the table with the pointed end toward you.

2 Starting from the bottom center peg, stretch a turquoise band up to the bottom left peg.

3 From the bottom center peg again, stretch a pink rubber band up to the second left peg.

4 From the bottom left peg, stretch a turquoise band up to the second center peg.

5 From the second center peg, stretch a turquoise band up to the third left peg.

6 From the second left peg stretch a pink band up to the third center peg.

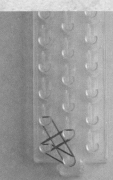

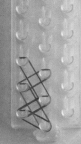

7 Look at your loom. You should see a zig-zag pattern forming for each color.

8 Continue building each zig-zag (one for pink and one for turquoise) up the loom until you reach the end.

9 When you get to the end, make a cap band (see page 13) from a pink rubber band and place it on the last peg (left corner).

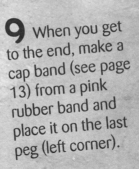
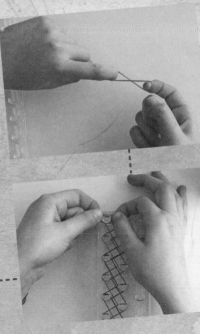

10 Turn the loom around so that the pointed end is away from you.

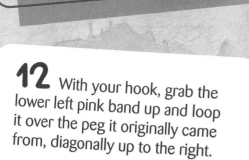

11 Use crochet hook to reach down the first peg, stretching the cap band out of the way and grabbing the turquoise band below it. Hold the cap band so that it does not come off and lift the turquoise band up and out of the peg. You will loop it over the peg it came from originally, diagonally up to the left.

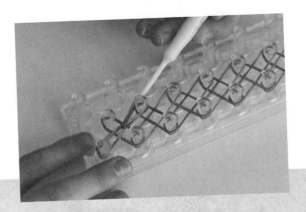

12 With your hook, grab the lower left pink band up and loop it over the peg it originally came from, diagonally up to the right.

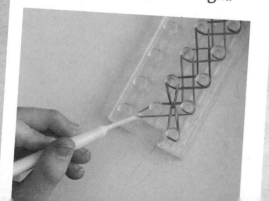

13 Continue hooking and looping up the loom until you reach the last peg.

CONTINUED →

14 Insert crochet hook down into the last peg and out to the side. Hook a pink rubber band on and, holding one end of the band with your fingers, pull the other end back up through the peg with the hook (a). Run the crochet hook through the loop you are holding in your hand (b) and push both ends of the band onto the thickest part of your crochet handle. Pull the bracelet off of the loom (c).

a

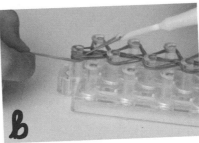

b

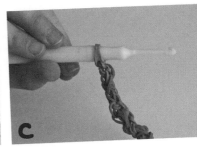

c

15 Place the loom in front of you with the arrow pointed away from you. Create an extension by looping five bands up one side of the loom (three turquoise and two pink, alternating the colors).

16 Take the loop from the end of the bracelet that you removed from the loom and loop it over the last peg of your extension.

17 Use the crochet hook to hook and loop the bands of the extension together.

18 Attach a c-clip to the last loop on the extension.

19 Stretch the bands that are around the handle of your crochet hook and attach the c-clip to it, sliding the crochet hook out.

What You Need:

✓ Paper clip
✓ 75–100 rubber bands (all approximately the same size)

Necklace

Make this fun and chunky necklace to wear with all your other rubber band bling. An easy project for when your friends come over, great for camp, and perfect for sleepovers!

1 Insert two rubber bands through the center of the paper clip.

2 Grab the ends of the two rubber bands and bring them together so they are touching.

3 Insert two rubber bands through the loop created by the first two rubber bands.

4 Grab the ends of the two rubber bands you just inserted and bring them together so they are touching.

5 Repeat steps 3 and 4 until you've reached a length you are happy with.

6 Clip the loops of the final rubber band through the paper clip. That's it!

Ring

If you can make a single pattern rubber band bracelet, you can make a ring too! Simply make it a lot shorter and your fingers will be stylin', too.

What You Need:
- ✓ C-clip
- ✓ 8 small rubber bands

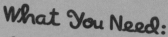

1 Flatten a rubber band between your fingers and insert it through a c-clip.

2 Holding the first rubber band in the shape of the letter "C" flatten a second rubber band and insert it through the two loops of the first rubber band.

3 Repeat step 2 for the remaining rubber bands.

4 Connect the last rubber band into the c-clip.

IT'S A SNAP

Feel like giving yourself a manicure, but can't get the top off your bottle of nail polish? Wrap a rubber band around the lid to help your grip. Still too tough? Wrap a few bands around the bottle for double gripping power!

Earrings

What You Need:

- ✓ Thick cardboard
- ✓ Scissors
- ✓ 2 fishhook earring wires
- ✓ 40–50 small rubber bands
- ✓ Craft knife*
- ✓ Round-nose pliers

*Ask an adult to help you use the craft knife.

You already have a collection of bracelets, so why not make some fun earrings to match all that arm jewelry! Be sure to use thick cardboard—if it's too thin, the rubber bands will make it bend.

1 Cut cardboard into two rectangles, each 1 x 1¼".

2 Wrap rubber bands around the width of the cardboard until full.

3 Wrap four bands around the length of the cardboard.

4 Use craft knife to poke a hole in the top of the rectangle, about ¼ inch from the top.

5 Insert fishhook earring wire into the hole and bend to close with round-nose pliers.

6 Repeat steps 2–5 for second earring.

Chain Belt

Dress up a boring outfit with little more than a chain of rubber bands and some colorful pony beads! Add your own flair with fun charms, too!

What You Need:
- ✓ 10–15 rubber bands
- ✓ 120–140 pony beads
- ✓ 1 large button or belt bead

1 Create a rubber band chain by looping several together. You will add more as you build your belt.

2 Begin threading beads onto the rubber band chain, leaving the first rubber band in the chain bead-free.

3 You can tie knots in the rubber bands as you go along to use as spacers if you like. To use fewer beads, space them out by tying a knot between each one.

4 Continue adding beads and rubber bands until you've reached the desired length.

5 Return to the first rubber band and shorten the loop opening by tying a knot. The loop should be smaller than the large button, but large enough for it to stretch so the button can fit through to close your belt.

6 At the end of your belt, cut the last rubber band so that you have two ends rather than a loop.

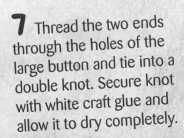

7 Thread the two ends through the holes of the large button and tie into a double knot. Secure knot with white craft glue and allow it to dry completely.

8 To wear belt, wrap around your waist and push the button through the open loop.

snap **FACT!**

According to Guinness World Records, the longest rubber band chain was created by Allison Coach, in Chesterfield Township, Michigan. It measured 1.32 miles long and that was before stretching it!

Pencil Can

Dress up your homework desk with rubber bands! Make a colorful striped pencil holder by covering a clean, recycled metal can with several different colored rubber bands. Start from the bottom and add one rubber band at a time, pushing them flush with each other to create a uniform look.

snap FACT!

The U.S. Postal Service is the largest user of rubber bands in the world. They use millions of pounds of rubber bands every year to sort and deliver piles of mail.

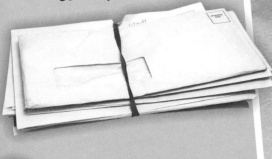

Memo Board

Use wide, colorful rubber bands and a plastic freestanding frame to create a fun memo board to hold pens, notes, money, and other important items. Simply wrap 4–6 wide rubber bands around the frame and insert your stuff!

Trading Card Organizer

Keep all of your favorite trading cards within arm's reach and eye view! All you need is a piece of foam core or an old corkboard (and some rubber bands, of course!). Wrap rubber bands vertically around the board, and then wrap some more horizontally, creating a crisscross pattern. Tuck your favorite cards in between the bands. That's it!

In a Pinch Bookmark

Don't dog-ear that page—use a rubber band instead! Simply stretch a rubber band around the section of the book you have already read. Presto—instant bookmark!

NOTEBOOK

What You Need:

✓ 2 sheets 4½ x 6" card stock

✓ 4–5 sheets 8½ x 11" white paper

✓ Craft stick

✓ Rubber band

✓ Hole puncher

✓ Scissors or paper cutter

These easy-to-make do-it-yourself notebooks are great for doodling, taking notes, or even keeping a diary. They also make great gifts for friends, are perfect for party favors, or a party craft.

1 Cut each sheet of white paper into quarters (creating four 4¼ x 5½" pieces of paper from each sheet).

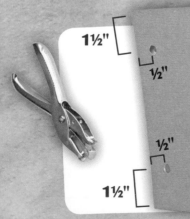

2 Stack both card stock sheets together and use hole puncher to create two holes for your binding. The holes should be about 1½ inches from the top and the bottom and at least ½ inch from the edge of the card stock so that holes won't tear.

1½"

½"

½"

1½"

3 Line up one sheet of your white paper inside your card stock book covers. Use holes to guide you and punch holes on the white sheet.

4 Use that white sheet as your template and punch holes in remaining white sheets.

5 Place white sheets between card stock front and back cover, and line up all the holes.

6 Insert the end of a rubber band into the top hole from the back of your book.

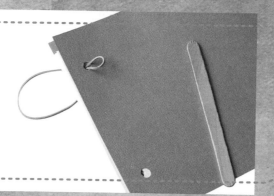

7 Insert the top of the craft stick into the loop of the rubber band.

8 At the back of the book, stretch the rubber band down to the second hole and insert it into the hole coming out the front of the book.

9 Insert the bottom of the craft stick into the loop of the rubber band.

Write Away!

snap FACT!

According to rubber band folklore, rubber (the main ingredient in a rubber band!) was "discovered" by Christopher Columbus in Haiti where he saw natives playing with balls made from the sap of a tree called "cau-uchu." And you probably thought he only "discovered" America!

Cheater Chopsticks

Do you have trouble using chopsticks? Make your own "cheater" chopsticks using a rubber band and a scrap of paper!

What You Need:

✓ 1 pair of chopsticks
✓ Scrap of paper
✓ 1 rubber band

1 Hold the chopsticks side by side and wrap a rubber band tightly around the top to hold them together. They should be tight enough so they won't come apart, but not so tight that you have trouble opening them.

2 Fold your piece of paper into a tight wad. Insert the wad of paper in between the two chopsticks, positioning it just below the rubber band.

3 You have created a spring action that allows you to hold the chopsticks with one hand and squeeze the open ends with your fingers. Let the banquet begin!

What You Need:

✓ 1 key
✓ 1 rubber band

KEY HOLDER

Who needs a key chain, when all you need is a rubber band? This simple (and we mean simple!) fix will help you keep track of your keys wherever you may be!

1 Thread the rubber band through the hole in the key.

2 Loop one end of the rubber band through the other end.

3 Pull tight. That's it!

EXTRA TWIST! You can now loop the rubber band around your wrist so you don't misplace your key when you are out and about. Or you can hang the key on a hook so you don't misplace it at home.

Stuff that Goes

Rubber Band Ball

Boiiiinnnng! What could be more fun than a bouncy ball made of rubber bands? And they are so easy to make!

1 Crumple up a piece of aluminum foil into a small ball.

2 Begin wrapping rubber bands around the ball. Space the bands evenly so that one side doesn't become larger than the others.

3 Keep wrapping until your ball is the size you want.

4 You will need to use larger rubber bands as your ball gets bigger.

5 Bounce away!

snap FACT!

According to Guinness World Records, the largest rubber band ball was created by Joel Waul in Lauderhill, Florida. It weighs 9,032 pounds, is more than eight feet tall, and took more than 700,000 rubber bands to create!

Cup Rocket Launcher

Two plastic cups and some rubber bands are all you will need to launch your own rocket right there in your living room. Try different-sized cups to see what flies the highest!

What You Need:

✓ 2 small plastic cups

✓ 5 or more rubber bands

✓ Markers for decorating (optional)

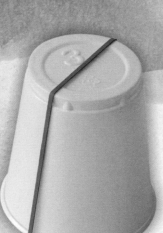

1 Wrap a rubber band around one cup, going from the top of the cup to the bottom.

2 Wrap a second rubber band around the cup in the same fashion, only this time crossing the other band.

3 Use remaining rubber bands to wrap around the body to secure the first two in place. You can use different colors, which act as a decoration as well! This is your rocket.

4 If you like, use markers to decorate the second cup, which is your launch pad. Draw flames to illustrate the rocket taking off!

5 Place the cup without the rubber bands (launch pad) upside down on the table or floor.

6 Place the rubber-banded cup (rocket) on top of the "launch pad" cup so that the rubber bands at the open end of the cup rest on the solid bottom of the launch pad.

7 Holding the sides of the rocket, push down over the launch pad, stretching the rubber bands. Release the rocket and watch it fly!

IT'S A SNAP

Keep your glasses or sunglasses in place by making a rubber band chain and looping the ends around the earpieces of your glasses.

Rubber Band Powered CAR

Ready, set, go! Get together with your friends and make these rubber band powered cars from a cardboard tube and recycled CD's. Wind them up over and over again to see who wins the most races!

What You Need:

- ✓ Heavy 12-inch cardboard tube (from aluminum foil works great)
- ✓ 1 wooden dowel 6 x ³⁄₁₆"
- ✓ 1 wooden dowel 9 x ³⁄₁₆"
- ✓ 4 recycled CDs
- ✓ 4 wooden craft spools 1 x ¾"
- ✓ 2 drinking straws
- ✓ 4 large buttons
- ✓ 20 standard rubber bands
- ✓ 1 large paper clip
- ✓ Hot-glue gun*
- ✓ Scissors
- ✓ Hole punch
- ✓ White craft glue
- ✓ Paint (optional)

*Ask an adult to help you use the hot-glue gun.

EXTRA TWIST!

If you would like to decorate your car, paint the cardboard tube and set aside to dry.

1 Use hot glue to attach a spool to the center of each CD (be sure they are centered!). It's easiest if you stand your spool up on the table and place the CD over the top so you can see if it's centered.

2 Hot-glue buttons to the other side of the CDs as hubcaps. This also keeps the axle from coming through.

3 Use hole punch to create a hole for the axle on one side of the cardboard tube.

4 Create another hole on the other side of the cardboard tube, using a ruler to make sure they are the same distance from the end of the tube. HINT: An easy way to line up the holes in the axles to make sure they are even is to loop a rubber band around the full length of the cardboard tube. Place the rubber band over the center of one hole and use the rubber band as a guide for placing the rest of the holes!

5 Repeat these steps at the other end of the tube, again using a ruler to make sure they align with the first axle.

6 Insert the 6-inch dowel into the holes at one end of the tube. Center the dowel and cut a drinking straw to create "stoppers" between the hole and the spool on the CD. Ours measure approximately one inch each for the front axle.

7 Thread the straws onto both ends of the wooden dowel.

8 Insert the ends of the dowel into the spools on the wheels.

9 If you are satisfied with everything and your axles turn freely, remove the dowel from spool, add some white craft glue to the inside of the spool and replace the dowel.

CONTINUED →

10 Repeat these steps with the back axle and the 9-inch wooden dowel. Your drinking straw stoppers will be a little longer on the back due to the longer axle, approximately 2¼ inches.

11 Use 3–4 rubber bands to make a chain.

12 Loop the first rubber band in the chain around the front axle inside the cardboard tube and run the entire chain through the loop; pull it tight.

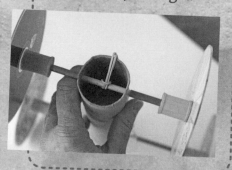

13 Attach a large paper clip to the end of the rubber band chain and drop it down into the tube. Reach into the back end of the cardboard tube to retrieve the paper clip.

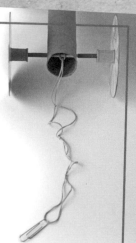

14 Clip it to the end of the cardboard tube. The length of the rubber band chain should be about the same length as the cardboard tube, so if it's too long, shorten the chain by one band.

15 Finally, give your wheels added traction by attaching rubber bands around the CD wheels, four on each wheel.

16 To wind up the car, hold the car with the back axle toward you and turn the front wheels counterclockwise. The rubber band chain will wrap around the front axle and get tighter. When it's tight, place the car on the ground and watch it go!

What You Need:

- ✓ 8 x 10" piece of sturdy cardboard
- ✓ Duct tape
- ✓ 1 standard rubber band
- ✓ Scissors

Rubber Band Powered BOAT

You can make your very own paddleboat with just a few supplies! Have races in the swimming pool or set sail in the tub.

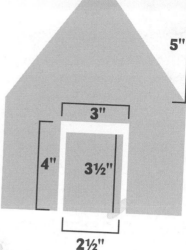

1 From the bottom of the cardboard, cut out a section about three inches wide and four inches high.

2 Cut the top of the cardboard into a triangular shape (about five inches high).

3 For the paddle, trim the rectangular piece that you just cut out down to 2½ x 3½".

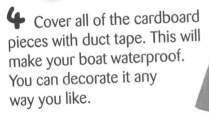

4 Cover all of the cardboard pieces with duct tape. This will make your boat waterproof. You can decorate it any way you like.

5 Wrap the rubber band once around the outside of the two long strips at the end of the boat.

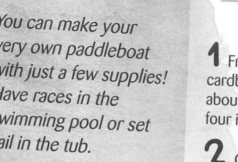

6 Insert the rectangular piece in between the rubber band in the rectangular opening.

7 Wind the paddle several times which will twist up the rubber band.

8 Place the boat in the water and let it go! The paddle will turn pushing the boat through the water.

Marshmallow Catapult

Talk about fun! Whether your target is a homemade bull's-eye or your friend's mouth, catapulting marshmallows high into the air with this homemade gadget is a blast!

1 Stack two craft sticks together and tightly wrap two of the rubber bands around one end.

2 Stack remaining seven craft sticks together and wrap one rubber band around one end, and another rubber band around the opposite end.

3 Insert the larger stack of craft sticks into the open end of the two craft sticks. Slide it in as far as it will go.

4 Secure the large stack with two more rubber bands in a crisscross fashion.

5 Place the spoon on the top craft stick so the neck and bowl are supported. Insert the end of the spoon handle into the crisscrossed rubber bands.

6 Secure the neck of the spoon to the stick using an additional rubber band.

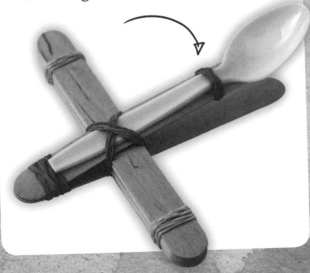

7 To play, hold each side of the base of the catapult with one hand. Place a marshmallow in the spoon bowl and depress it with your finger. Let go and watch the marshmallows fly!

IT'S A SNAP

Improve your grip by wrapping the handle of your baseball bat with rubber bands. The bands will keep your hands from slipping, even on hot, sweaty days!

BOING! **Q:** What's the longest word in the dictionary?

A: Rubber-band... because it stretches!

BOW and ARROWS

1 With an adult's help, fill a heavy-bottomed saucepan halfway with water. Add several craft sticks and bring to a boil for 30 minutes. Remove from heat and allow them to sit in the hot water for 30 minutes.

2 Drain the craft sticks and give them a quick rinse in warm water to make them easier to handle.

3 Carefully bend the craft sticks into arch shapes and place into the glass container, using the curve of the glass to form the bow. Allow the sticks to dry overnight.

Move over Katniss! Bring out your inner archer with these easy to make (and even more fun to shoot) bows and arrows. Make them with your friends and have a contest to see whose goes the farthest!

EXTRA TWIST! Sometimes the craft sticks crack when you curve them. Be sure to boil extra craft sticks just in case some break.

4 Remove sticks from container and use a craft knife to cut small notches at the end of each stick, about an inch from the end. Cut notches on both sides of each end for a total of four notches.

5 For each bow, cut open a rubber band. Tie one end of a rubber band around the end of the craft stick, lining up the rubber band in the notches.

EXTRA TWIST!
Decorate your bows with colorful markers.

6 Stretch the other end of the rubber band to the other end of the craft stick and tie in a knot.

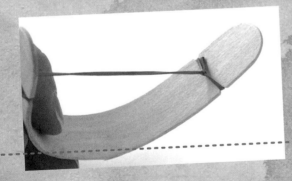

7 Trim off the excess and add some white craft glue to the knot. Allow the glue to dry completely.

8 To play, cut one end off of each cotton swab. Hold the bow in your hand and place the cut end of the cotton swab in the center of the rubber band. Pull the rubber band and cotton swab back and let go to release your flying arrow!

Slingshot

Get in some target practice or have competitions with your friends to see who can shoot the farthest. All you need to do is build a simple slingshot from rubber bands and a sturdy stick.

What You Need:

✓ Y-shaped sturdy branch
✓ Craft knife*
✓ 12 regular rubber bands
✓ 1 wide rubber band
✓ Duct tape
✓ Cutting board
✓ Hole punch

*Ask an adult to help you use the craft knife.

1 Use a craft knife to carve a v-shaped notch on the outside edge of each tine on your branch, about 1½ inches from the top.

2 Create a rubber band chain from four of the regular rubber bands. Repeat for a second chain. Set the remaining four rubber bands aside.

3 Cut the wide rubber band in half to create two equal pieces.

4 Lay one of the wide rubber band strips over the carved notch on one of the tines. Wrap one of the rubber band chains around the tine, enclosing the wide rubber band inside. Wrap the rubber band chain completely around the wide band and tie in three or four knots to secure.

5 Repeat this step for the other tine.

6 To create the pouch, measure and cut an 8-inch strip of duct tape.

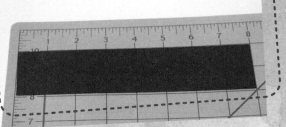

7 Fold the tape in half, creating a 4-inch piece of double-sided tape. Use a craft knife or scissors to trim the tape into an almond-shaped pouch.

8 Punch a hole on both sides of the pouch, about ½ inch from the edges.

9 Use the remaining four rubber bands to create two chains using two bands for each chain.

10 Thread one end of the wide rubber band through one of the holes on the pouch.

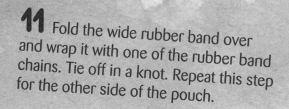

11 Fold the wide rubber band over and wrap it with one of the rubber band chains. Tie off in a knot. Repeat this step for the other side of the pouch.

12 Make a quick ball from wadded up duct tape and place it into the center of the pouch. Pinch the pouch so that the ball is inside, held by your fingers. Pull the pouch back while holding the hande of the branch with the other hand. Aim and release!

Catapult Paper Airplane

What You Need:

✓ 8½ x 11" sheet of paper
✓ Hole punch
✓ Rubber band
✓ Pencil
✓ Markers for decorating (optional)

Sure, everyone knows how to throw a paper airplane, but did you know that you can catapult one into flight? All you need is a paper airplane, a rubber band, and a pencil!

1 Fold paper in half lengthwise and crease the center. Open the paper up again.

2 Fold the upper left-hand corner down, lining up the edge of the paper with the center crease. Repeat this for the upper right-hand corner.

3 Fold the left side of the paper down toward the center of the paper again, lining up the straight edge with the center crease. Repeat on the right-hand side.

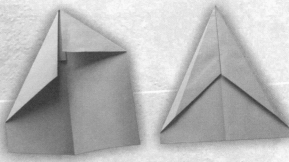

4 Fold paper along the center crease so that the left- and right-hand creases are on the outside.

5 Fold one side of the paper down, starting as close to the airplane's point as you can. Repeat for the other side.

6 Hold the airplane as if you were going to launch it. Use the hole punch to make a hole at approximately that same spot.

7 Thread a rubber band through the hole.

8 Thread one loop end of the rubber band through the other loop end and pull tight.

9 Hold a pencil in front of you with your arm extended straight. The pencil tip should be pointing toward the floor.

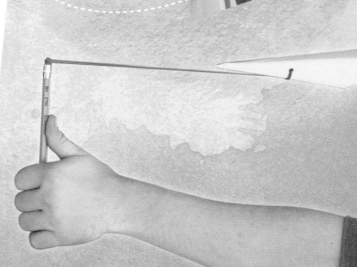

10 Loop the end of the rubber band around the eraser end of the pencil and pull the airplane back toward you.

11 When the rubber band is tight, release the airplane from your fingers and watch it fly!

Bobby Pin Launcher

Never underestimate the power of a rubber band and a few recycled items from around the house! You can use an empty cereal box or the back of a writing pad for this great project. Takes less than a minute to create and provides hours of launching fun!

What You Need:

✓ Thin recycled cardboard
✓ Bobby pin
✓ Rubber band

1 Cut cardboard into a circle with a tab sticking out (like an apostrophe!).

2 Thread rubber band through the bobby pin.

3 Hold the bobby pin with one hand and hook the tab of the cardboard inside the open loop of the rubber band.

4 Holding the cardboard flat, pull it back toward you, stretching out the rubber band.

5 Release the cardboard and watch it spin as it flies!

BOING!

Q: What did the burglar get when he robbed the rubber band factory?

A: A long stretch in jail!

48

4 Ways to Shoot a Rubber Band With Your Fingers

Whether you're shooting rubber bands for distance or accuracy, here are four different ways to make your fingers work for you!

The Back Launch

1 Loop one end of the rubber band over the tip of your ring finger and the other end over the tip of your thumb. Bend ring finger down toward your palm.

2 Bend index finger down and underneath the center of the rubber band.

3 Stretch rubber band up by lifting index finger, keeping thumb and ring finger in original position.

4 Release rubber band from ring finger to launch. The rubber band will fly backward—be careful that you don't shoot it into your face!

The Classic

1 Loop the rubber band around your index finger.

2 With one end of the rubber band at the top of your index finger, use the index finger of your other hand to stretch the rubber band back.

3 Release the rubber band with the hand in the back to launch.

The Wrap

1 Loop rubber band over tip of pinky finger. Touch pinky finger to the palm of your hand, trapping rubber band inside.

2 Wrap other end of rubber band around your thumb and hook onto the tip of your index finger.

3 Point your index finger where you want to shoot and let go of the rubber band with your pinky to launch.

The Triangle

1 Loop one end of the rubber band around the tip of your index finger.

2 With the index finger and middle finger of your other hand, stretch the band back until you have formed a triangle.

3 Aim and launch!

Never aim a rubber band at someone's face!

Geo Board

What You Need:

- ✓ Corkboard
- ✓ Pushpins
- ✓ Ruler
- ✓ Rubber bands
- ✓ White craft glue (optional)

1 Use a ruler to measure two inches from the top of your corkboard, and two inches from the left side. Place your first pushpin in this spot.

2 Place more pushpins, two inches apart, across the top of your corkboard and then create a new row two inches below the first.

Create your own toy with a corkboard, some pushpins, and (what else?) a handful of rubber bands. You will have loads of fun making all sorts of shapes and patterns on your very own geo board.

3 Continue row after row until you have made a grid.

4 If you want the pins to be more permanent, add a dab of glue to each one before you push it in. Allow the pins to dry completely.

5 Now it's time to create shapes by looping the ends of the bands over the tops of the pushpins. See how many different shapes you can make!

Rubber Band Stamping

Make pretty stationery, decorate a frame, or even design a T-shirt using your own homemade stamps! All you need is something for a base and some rubber bands!

1 Choose your rubber bands and objects to use as a base.

2 Wrap as many rubber bands around your objects as you like.

3 To use, simply press your stamp into an ink pad then press onto the thing you want to decorate.

It's important for your dog to have a license tag, a vaccination tag, and an I.D. tag attached to his collar. But did you know that all that clatter can hurt his ears? Simply wrap a rubber band around the tags, holding them together. No more noise and happy dog!

Snap Painting

This is a super fun activity, but be warned...it's messy! So be sure to wear a smock and cover your work surface—or better yet, do this outside!

What You Need:
✓ Cookie sheet
✓ Rubber bands in various widths
✓ Craft paint
✓ Paint brushes or sponge applicators
✓ Paper
✓ Tape

1 Wrap rubber bands around the length of the cookie sheet, spacing them about an inch apart.

2 Turn the cookie sheet over. Roll two pieces of tape and stick them to the back of the sheet. The tape will hold the cookie sheet in place on your work surface.

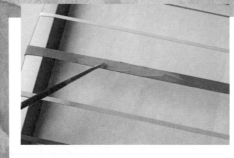

4 Paint a rubber band with craft paint.

3 Slide paper underneath the rubber bands onto the cookie sheet. Depending on the size of your cookie sheet you may need more than one piece of paper.

5 Lift the rubber band straight up and release. The paint will "snap" onto the paper.

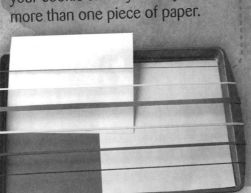

6 Repeat steps 4 and 5 with additional paint colors.

7 Continue painting and snapping until you are happy with your artwork!

DYED EGGS

Add some pizzazz to your traditional dyed eggs this Easter with a handful of rubber bands!

What You Need:

✓ Boiled eggs with shells on
✓ Food coloring
✓ Vinegar
✓ Water
✓ Cups
✓ Spoons
✓ Paper towels
✓ Rubber bands

1 Fill each cup with water. Add two tablespoons of white vinegar and several drops of food coloring. Stir each color with its own spoon.

2 Wrap rubber bands around the boiled eggs. Not too tight! You don't want the eggs to crack.

3 Lower a wrapped egg into colored water with a spoon. Leave in the dye for 3–4 minutes.

4 Lift egg out of colored water and drain on paper towels.

5 When dry, remove rubber bands.

53

What You Need:

✓ White shirt
✓ Marbles
✓ Rubber bands
✓ Clothing dye (like Rit dye)
✓ Protective gloves
✓ 5-gallon bucket or large plastic storage container

Easy Tie-Dye Designs

Want to add some personality to a plain white T-shirt? Tie-dyeing is the ticket! With just a few materials, you can design a wild, colorful creation of your own. So grab a few marbles and a handful of rubber bands, and let's get busy making these cool designs.

1 First wash and dry your shirt, but don't use fabric softener, which can sometimes cause problems with the dye sticking.

2 For a starburst pattern, place a marble inside the shirt where you want the center of the starburst to be. From the outside of the shirt, wrap a rubber band tightly around the marble.

3 Wrap another rubber band around the shirt about an inch below the marble. Repeat this two more times.

4 For circles, simply place marbles inside the shirt and from the outside of the shirt, wrap a rubber band tightly around each marble.

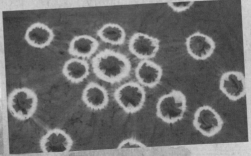

5 For stripes, tightly wrap rubber bands around the entire width of the shirt.

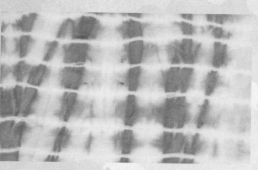

6 With an adult's help, follow the instructions on the clothing dye. Be sure you follow all safety tips and precautions, like wearing protective gloves.

7 When the fabric is dry, remove the rubber bands and…wow!

EXTRA TWIST!
Don't have a T-shirt? Try these same techniques with a bandana, a plain tote-bag, a sweatshirt, even a pair of boxers!

IT'S A SNAP

To keep the cuff of your pants from getting caught in your gears, gather the pant cuff close to your leg and wrap with rubber bands!

Luminarias

Need a gift for Mother's Day or for your favorite teacher? Make a couple of these beautiful luminarias and you are sure to make someone's heart glow!

What You Need:

✓ Recycled glass jars
✓ Rubber bands
✓ Spray paint
✓ Scissors
✓ Scrubber sponge
✓ Paper towels
✓ Tea light candles

1 Wash and dry jars, making sure that all labels have been removed.

2 Wrap jars with rubber bands. Crisscross them in any pattern that you like.

3 Apply two thin coats of spray paint to each jar, allowing them to dry for twenty minutes between coats.

EXTRA TWIST! Parental participation is suggested for handling spray paint.

4 Carefully lift edge of rubber bands and cut with scissors to remove.

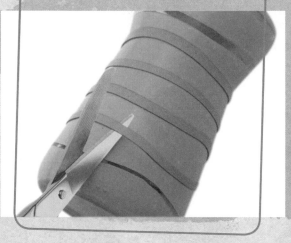

5 Use a damp scrubber sponge to remove any extra spray from inside the jar. Wipe out with paper towel.

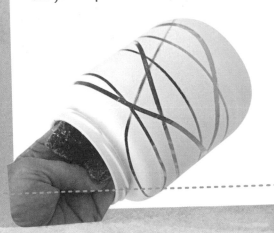

6 Add a tea light candle and you are ready to glow!

EXTRA TWIST! LED tea lights are available at most dollar stores and discount department stores and are much safer than regular tea light candles.

What You Need:

✓ 23 turquoise rubber bands

✓ 8 white rubber bands

✓ 5 black rubber bands

✓ Loom

✓ Crochet hook

We have made ours with turquoise, white, and black rubber bands, but you can substitute any colors you like!

Popsicle Charm

Did you know you can make more than bracelets with a rubber band loom? This fun charm is a little tricky, but with some practice, you'll get the hang of it. Once you start making them, you will find plenty of uses for them—attach one to a key chain, dangle one from your backpack, make them for your friends. They are, of course, great additions to your rubber band bracelets, too!

1 Place your loom on the table with the pointed end toward you.

3 From the bottom left peg, stretch a turquoise DB up to the second peg. Repeat this two more times for a total of three DB's up the left side.

2 Starting from the bottom center peg, stretch a turquoise DB (see page 13) up to the bottom left peg.

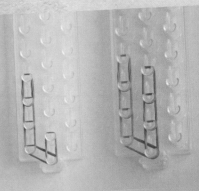

4 Return to the bottom center peg and stretch a turquoise DB up one peg. Repeat this two more times for a total of three DB's up the middle.

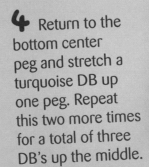

58

5 Return to the bottom center peg and stretch a turquoise DB up to the bottom right peg.

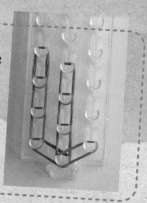

6 From the bottom right peg, stretch a turquoise DB up to the second peg. Repeat this two more times for a total of three DB's up the right side.

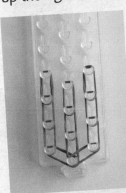

7 From the last turquoise band, stretch a white DB up one peg for each left, right, and center pegs.

8 From the center white band, stretch a black DB up one peg. Repeat for one more black DB.

9 Turn the loom around so that the pointed end is away from you.

10 Place a turquoise brace band (see page 13) in a triangular fashion beginning from the second center peg from the top down one peg left and right.

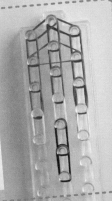

11 Going down to the next open center peg, add another turquoise brace band as in step 10. Repeat once more for a third turquoise brace band.

12 Go down one more peg and add a white brace band below the three turquoise brace bands.

CONTINUED →

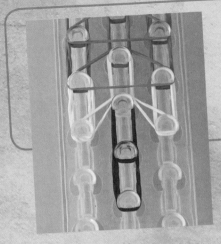

13 For only the white triangle brace band, use your hook to stretch the bottom of the triangle up and over the peg where the top point of the triangle is. Leave the turquoise brace bands as is.

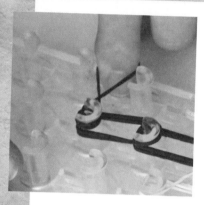

14 Add a black triple cap band (see page 13) to the bottom black peg.

15 Add white triple cap bands to the bottom left and right of the white brace band.

16 To hook the charm, begin on the bottom left peg. With the hook away from you, insert the hook down into the bottom left peg. Use the back of your crochet hook to pull the cap band and brace band toward you and use the hook to grab the bottom two white bands.

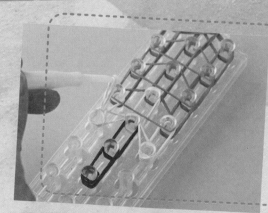

17 Hold your cap band in place with your free hand and pull the hooked bottom bands up through the peg and loop them over the next peg up.

18 Continue hooking and looping bands, using the back of the hook to pull the brace band out of the way before hooking the bottom two bands. Work your way up the left side, hooking the final left peg up and over the top center peg.

19 Repeat the hooking process for the center and right rows.

20 Turn the loom around so that the top of the popsicle is closest to you. Insert crochet hook down through the top peg and tilt it out to the side. Be sure that you have cleared all the bands on that top peg.

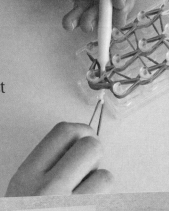

21 Loop a turquoise band over the hook and stretch it tight. Carefully pull the crochet hook back up through the center of the peg while holding the loose end of the rubber band with your other hand.

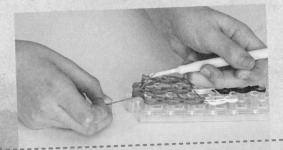

22 Place the hook through the opposite end of the rubber band, up and over the hook. Pull the end of the band that is on the hook through the other end of the band and pull it tight to make the charm's hanger.

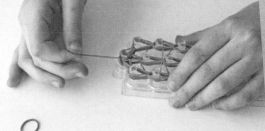

23 Insert the crochet hook down through that same top peg again and use it to pull the charm up off of the peg and remove it from the loom.

What You Need:

- ✓ Wide rubber bands in various sizes
- ✓ White craft glue
- ✓ Glitter
- ✓ Construction paper
- ✓ Cotton swabs

Glitter Art

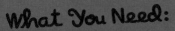

Who knew you could use rubber bands to create a piece of glittery, shiny art! The design is completely up to you. Make a picture or an abstract sculpture, all by using rubber bands, glue, and glitter.

1 Arrange your rubber bands on construction paper in the design you choose.

2 One by one, lift each rubber band and line the bottom of it with glue then gently press it in place on the paper.

3 Let the glue dry for at least 20 minutes.

4 Add some glue in the center of each rubber band.

5 Spread the glue around inside the rubber bands with the tip of your finger or a cotton swab.

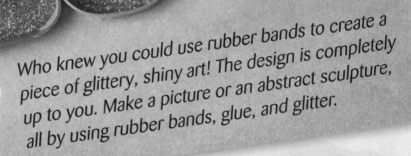

6 Carefully sprinkle glitter inside each rubber band on top of the glue. Tap out the excess. If using multiple colors, do one color at a time, tap out, return excess to container, then move on to the next color.

HARP 😎

Don't throw out your empty shoeboxes. Instead make a fun musical harp using a handful of rubber bands! Try different width bands to make different sounds.

1 Wrap approximately 8–10 rubber bands around the entire box, spacing them out so they aren't touching.

2 Pluck rubber bands with your fingers to make sounds.

3 To play as a harp, run fingers down the instrument's "strings" starting from the top and gently dragging fingers over all the bands toward the bottom.

EXTRA TWIST!

Still have the lid from your shoebox? Make a second harp from the lid so you and a friend can make music together!

BOING! **Q:** What kind of band never performs?

A: A rubber band!

Rubber-Band Band

Explore all the different sounds that you can make with ordinary household containers and different sized rubber bands. When strumming away at these homemade instruments, you'll notice that depending on the width and length of the bands used, each produces a different sound. The containers make a difference, too, so be sure to try various types including glass, metal, cardboard, and plastic!

What You Need:
✓ Household containers (pans, plastic storage containers, bowls, jars, cups, mugs, etc.)
✓ Rubber bands of various width and length

1 Wrap rubber bands around the container from top to bottom.

2 Strum each instrument by gently lifting a rubber band and releasing it.

Hmm...

✓ What container made your favorite sound?

✓ Did any container make a sound that surprised you?

✓ Can you figure out how to play a song?

Guitar

It's a classic! Children have been strumming on cardboard guitars with rubber band strings for as long as we can remember. The beauty of this project is that you can make this instrument from any recycled box you can find!

What You Need:

✓ Recycled cracker or cereal box
✓ Jar or cup (for tracing)
✓ Scissors
✓ 6–8 rubber bands
✓ Paint stir stick
✓ Clear shipping tape

EXTRA TWIST!
If you have a craft knife, a grown-up can help you use it to cut a circle out without opening up the box.

3 Cut the circle out.

1 Carefully open up your box at the seams.

2 Place cup in the center of the front flap of the box and trace it with a pen or pencil.

4 Tape the box back together.

5 Wrap the center of the box with rubber bands, spacing them evenly apart crossing over the circle.

6 Tape the paint stir stick to the back of the box.

Craft Stick KAZOO

Can you kazoo a kazoo? You can with a few supplies and these simple instructions! In minutes you'll be making music, so be sure to make extra for your friends!

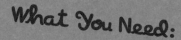

What You Need:

✓ 2 jumbo craft sticks
✓ 1 large, wide rubber band
✓ 2 regular rubber bands
✓ 1 drinking straw
✓ Paint for decorating (optional)

1 If you would like a colorful kazoo, paint both sides of the craft sticks and allow them to dry completely.

2 Stretch the wide rubber band over one of the craft sticks, lengthwise.

3 Cut two pieces from your drinking straw that measure 1½ inches each.

4 Slide one straw underneath the rubber band so that it runs perpendicular to the craft stick. The straw should be about ½ inch from the end of the stick.

5 Place the other straw at the other end of the craft stick, on top of the rubber band. This straw should also be about ½ inch from the end of the stick.

6 Place the second craft stick directly on top of the first one, covering both straws. Squeeze tightly so that the straws do not escape!

7 Wrap one of the regular rubber bands around the end of the sandwiched craft sticks. Repeat on the other end of the sticks with the second rubber band. Be sure that the rubber bands are snug.

8 Hold the kazoo with both hands and blow air into the center between the sticks. The vibration from that center rubber band will create sound!

Stuff to Try

Bundle of Energy

Oh, no! Not a science lesson! We bet that when you see how easy (and fun!) this lesson is, you'll be asking for more!

Energy is what makes things go, move, or work. A bicycle wouldn't move without the energy that your legs put on the pedals. A kite would not fly without the energy from the blowing wind.

What You Need:

✓ Ruler
✓ Rubber band
✓ Measuring tape
✓ Piece of paper
✓ Pen or pencil

Energy comes in two forms, potential and kinetic:

PE (potential energy) is energy that is stored, or "to be used."

KE (kinetic energy) is energy that is in motion, or "being used."

1 Place a ruler on the table, holding it with one hand so that it's standing on its side. The full length of the ruler should be touching the table surface, but the end of the ruler will be upright.

2 Loop one end of a rubber band around the end of the ruler where the measurements start.

3 Using your free hand, stretch the rubber band back along the top of the ruler, making note of what measurement you stretch it to. For example, if you stretched it to the 4-inch mark, keep that number in your head or ask a friend to write it down for you on your paper.

4 Release the rubber band, making sure no one is in your line of fire!

5 Use a measuring tape to find out how far your rubber band flew, starting from the end of the ruler that it launched from.

6 Record both the inch mark that you stretched the band to (this is the PE) and the distance to which the rubber band flew (the KE).

7 Repeat steps 2–6 several times, stretching the band a little more or less than in step 3, to observe the affect that PE has on KE.

EXTRA TWIST!
To get the most accurate results, keep the angle and the height of your ruler launch the same for each launch experiment.

Turn On the Heat

Please! Not another science lesson! Now that you have learned about the different forms of energy (on page 67), why not learn how energy can change the length of a rubber band?

(on page 67)

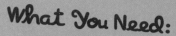

What You Need:

- ✓ Paper clip
- ✓ Rubber band
- ✓ Weight (we used a bottle opener)
- ✓ Hair dryer
- ✓ Ruler
- ✓ Scissors

1 Cut the rubber band to make it one long piece.

2 Tie one end of the rubber band to the paper clip.

3 Tie the other end of the rubber band to the weight. The weight should be heavy enough to stretch the rubber band out.

4 Have a friend hold the paper clip, suspending the weight from the rubber band.

5 Heat the rubber band with a hair dryer on the hot setting, moving the hair dryer nozzle up and down the band.

snap FACT!

Did you know that rubber bands last longer if you store them in the refrigerator? Brrr!

6 The energy from the heat of the hair dryer causes the rubber band to contract—or get smaller—pulling the weight up. We bet you thought the weight would pull the band down, didn't you?

Try this experiment with different weights and different sized bands. Use a ruler to measure the length of the band before and after heating it.

The Incredible Jumping Band

This simple trick gives the illusion of a rubber band jumping from one side of your hand to the other! Your friends will be wondering how you did that?

1 Hold your hand up in the air, palm facing you. Place the small rubber band over your pinky and ring fingers.

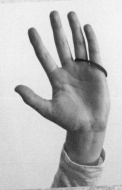

What You Need:
✓ 1 thin rubber band
✓ 1 small rubber band

2 Place the thin rubber band over your index finger. Twist it once and place it over your middle finger. Twist it again and place over your ring finger. Finally, twist it again and place over your pinky.

3 Keep your fingers together and straight up. Bring your thumb over across your palm and tuck it under the small rubber band. Bring your thumb back to its original position, stretching the rubber band with it.

4 With your thumb pointed straight up, fold your remaining fingers down toward your palm and tuck the tips of your fingers under the stretched small band.

5 Lift your fingers up and back into their original position, releasing your thumb from the band.

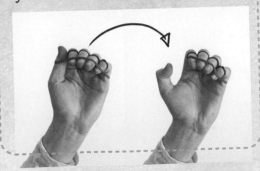

6 When your fingers return to the original position, the small rubber band will have moved from your pinky and ring finger over to your index and middle finger!

INCREDIBLE!

Make a Rubber Band DISAPPEAR

This is a fun trick to show to your younger brother or sister. They will be amazed that you started with two rubber bands and made one disappear!

What You Need:

✓ 1 medium rubber band

1 Steps 1–3 should be done away from view of your audience. Loop the rubber band around your left index finger and twist it into a figure eight, then loop the other end around your left thumb.

2 Insert your right index finger and thumb into the figure eight where your left finger and thumb are.

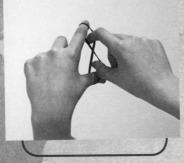

3 Stretch the band out using all four fingers. Keeping the band stretched, close your fingers and thumbs so they are touching each other. This should give the appearance of holding two stretched rubber bands.

4 Holding your fingers together, show your audience that you are holding "two" stretched rubber bands.

5 To demonstrate, keep your right thumb and finger together and separate your left thumb and finger. This will raise one side of the band up making it look like you have two separate bands. Close the left thumb and finger and open the right to demonstrate the other side. Remember to always keep one side, left or right, closed or your secret will be revealed!

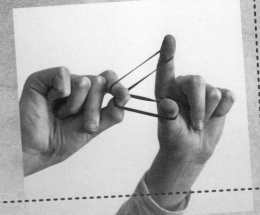

6 With band stretched out and both left and right fingers and thumbs touching, turn your hands toward you so that the band slips off your thumbs and completely onto your left and right index fingers. It will still look like you are holding two bands.

7 Turn your hands toward you to hide the rubber band inside your cupped hands. Say some magic words (abracadabra works!) and open your palm to reveal that you only have one rubber band left as the "other" band has mysteriously disappeared!

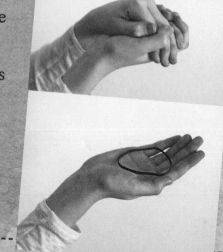

CAT'S CRADLE

This isn't a magic trick. It isn't an experiment. It isn't a craft. It's just plain fun!

What You Need:
✓ 1 medium rubber band

1 Place your palms together and slip a rubber band around your fingers.

2 Spread your fingers wide apart with the rubber band even with your knuckles.

3 Weave your fingers together as you bend your fingers in toward the center of your palms.

4 The rubber band should now be caught around each finger.

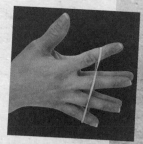

5 Now begin to fold your fingers in as you pull your hands apart.

6 Keep pulling your hands apart and you will see that the rubber band has formed a little ladder—or cat's cradle!

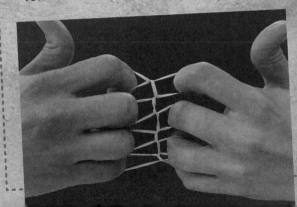

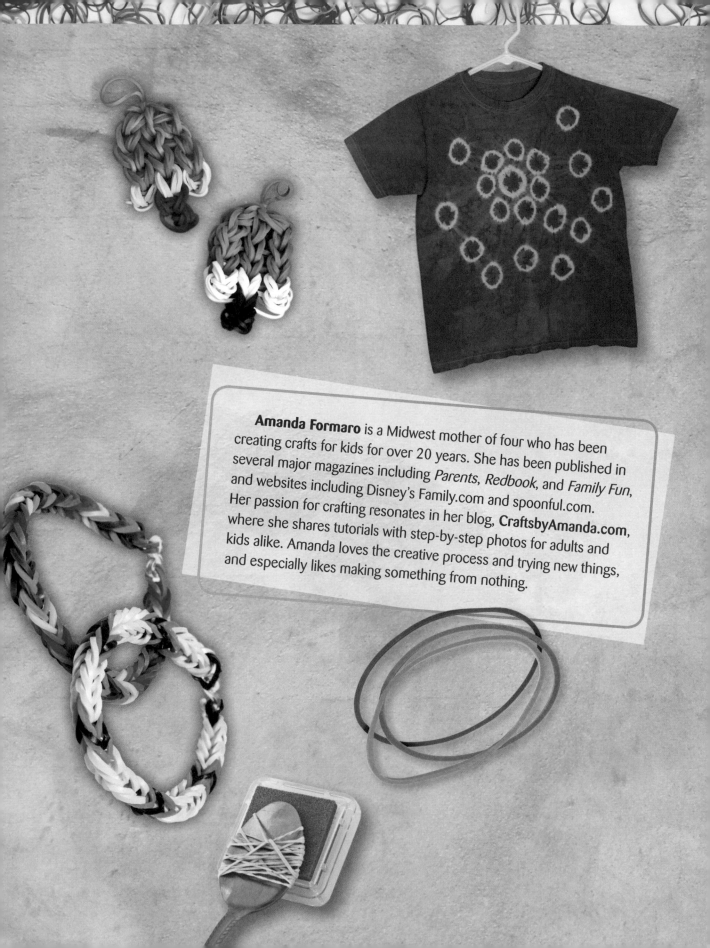

Amanda Formaro is a Midwest mother of four who has been creating crafts for kids for over 20 years. She has been published in several major magazines including *Parents*, *Redbook*, and *Family Fun*, and websites including Disney's Family.com and spoonful.com. Her passion for crafting resonates in her blog, **CraftsbyAmanda.com**, where she shares tutorials with step-by-step photos for adults and kids alike. Amanda loves the creative process and trying new things, and especially likes making something from nothing.